1

Easy Golf Etiquette

By Michael Thomas

Table Of Contents

Introduction

The sport of golf contains many rules of etiquette by which players are expected to conduct themselves during a round. Many of these rules are largely unwritten and unfamiliar to new or inexperienced golfers. It can be intimidating playing any sport when you aren't quite sure how to conduct yourself. But I'm here to tell you it doesn't have to be! By breaking the game of golf down into four key components, we can simplify the learning curve of these rules of etiquette.

In this guide we will discuss etiquette as it pertains to preparing for a round of golf, teeing off, playing shots within the fairway or rough, and putting on the green. Simple enough, right? We will also talk about how to handle ourselves when viewing a golf event as a spectator.

It may seem tedious at first, but the rules of etiquette in golf exist simply to keep the golf course operating smoothly and to make the round enjoyable and safe for you, your playing partners, and all of the other golfers you are sharing the course with.

Remember, it takes a little bit of practice to get the hang of things. Everyone makes mistakes at first. And that's ok! Keep learning and keep practicing and these rules of etiquette will start to come naturally to you as you continue to enjoy the game of golf!

Prior To The Round

Prepare Your Equipment

Before heading to the golf course, make sure you have everything you might need. Aside from the obvious things like clubs, balls, and tees, you may want to bring:

- Sunscreen
- Bug Spray
- Sunglasses
- Hat
- Towel
- Golf shoes
- Umbrella

Dress Appropriately

Different golf courses have different dress codes, but most public and private courses will require you to wear a collared shirt. Private courses may have stricter rules regarding bottoms as well. It's common for a course to list its dress code on its website, or if you are in doubt, simply call and ask!

Arrive Early

You'll want to allow yourself plenty of time to get ready at the golf course, so plan to arrive early. You may need to change into your golf shoes, pay green fees at the clubhouse, load your golf cart (if you are using one), hit some putts on the practice green, use the driving range, or stretch out. At a bare minimum, you will want to arrive 15 minutes before your tee time.

Be at the first tee box and ready to play five to ten minutes before your scheduled tee time. Some golf courses have an employee on the first tee box that will check your receipt and tell you when you can begin your round. This person is called a "starter" and is in charge of maintaining the pace of play, among several other things. The starter may also inform you of course specific rules or conditions. For example, if the course recently received a large amount of rain, the starter may inform you to stay on the cart paths.

Silence Your Phone

Before you head out to the first tee box, make sure your phone is set to silent. There is nothing more frustrating for you or your playing partners than a phone going off in the middle of a swing!

Maintain Your Temper

It hardly ever happens that everything goes your way during a round of golf. Getting angry rarely if ever helps you play better.

Don't yell, throw clubs, or pout. It's not going to help your game. It also makes for an uncomfortable outing for the people in your group. Nobody wants to play with someone who gets angry every time they hit a bad shot.

Remember, one of the reasons you are playing golf should be for fun! So enjoy yourself and try your best to brush off the miscues during a round.

On The Tee Box

Tee Off Order

In golf, a system called "honor" determines who has the right to tee off first. The player who had the lowest score on the previous hole is said to "have honors" and therefore gets to go first.

Obviously on the very first hole, you will need to determine a different way to decide the initial order. You can flip a coin, throw a tee in the air and see who it points closest to, or simply agree in a friendly manner.

If a course is busy and your group is falling behind the group ahead of you, you are encouraged to play "ready golf". This means whichever player is ready to hit first should do so, rather than strictly following honors. Ready golf speeds up the pace of play by allowing those who are ready to hit instead of waiting for someone who might not yet be prepared.

Remain Quiet And Still During Shots

When someone else is hitting, you should remain quiet and still from the time they address the ball to the time they finish their shot. Don't move around, as the player hitting may become distracted by seeing motion out of the corner of their eye.

Replace Divots

If your tee shot takes a large chunk of grass, also known as a "divot", out of the ground and the divot is retrievable, collect it and set it back over the bare spot. Some tee boxes will have a sand filled tool that you can sprinkle over the bare spot as well. This is especially common on par three holes where you are more likely to hit an iron and therefore create a divot. Also, try not to create any divots when taking practice swings, as this causes unnecessary damage to a tee box.

Don't Hit Until It's Safe

Before you tee off, make sure there aren't any players in the group ahead of you still within range. If you aren't quite sure if they are far enough out, it's better to wait. Once they move out of range, be ready to hit.

If you have a shorter hitter in your group and the players you are waiting on are out of this person's range, let them hit first. Once the group you are waiting on gets out of the way, the longer hitters can proceed with teeing off.

Yelling Fore!

If you do happen to hit an errant shot or you have underestimated how far away someone is, and your ball is headed towards them, yell "Fore!!" as loud as you can. This serves as a warning that a ball is incoming.

If you happen to hear someone yell "Fore!" in your direction, cover your head and duck down. Don't attempt to locate the ball because you won't have time. You want to protect your head in case the ball does strike you.

Playing Through

If there is a group of golfers behind you that is playing significantly faster than your group, allow them pass you by playing through. On the next tee box, let them tee off and go ahead of your group.

If the course is full and your group is already waiting on golfers ahead of you, then you should not let others play through. They will simply be stuck waiting just like you were, and nothing will be gained by allowing them through.

In The Fairway Or Rough

Order Of Play

In the fairway or rough, the player who is farthest from the hole is considered to be "out". This person is the player who gets to hit next.

Letting the player who is out hit first is a general rule, but this may be another opportunity to play ready golf in the fairway and rough. If you are not directly in front of another player who is out and you are ready to hit, go ahead and hit. You should also hit if you are ready and a further out player is still trying to locate a lost ball. The idea of ready golf is to reasonably forego strict order of play rules to speed of the pace of play.

Whatever order you hit in, try to never have two players in your group hitting at the exact same time.

Keep The Cart Out Of The Way

When you pull up to a ball in a motorized cart, make sure to park out of the way of both your potential swing path and ball flight. It's preferable to park to the side and slightly behind the ball. When someone else is hitting, be aware of any trees or other permanent objects on the course with which a ball could hit and ricochet back towards you.

As you approach greens, make sure to keep your cart a significant distance away. Remain on the cart path if there is one. Before you head out to chip and putt, park the cart to the side or behind the green. This makes for quicker exiting of the hole to clear it for the group behind you.

Limit Practice Swings

When it is your turn to hit, limit the number of practice swings you take to one or two. If you are falling behind the group ahead of you or holding up play for the group behind you, only take one practice swing at the most.

Search For Lost Balls

Keep your search for lost balls to a reasonable time. Please don't spend more than three minutes searching for a ball, and preferably even less time if the course is busy. If you can't find your ball within this amount of time, consider it lost and drop a ball (taking the appropriate penalty strokes).

If a player within your group is in a separate golf cart and has lost a ball you can help them look for it, just so long as your own ball is located reasonably close by. It's preferable that you hit your own shot first before you help someone in another golf cart find their lost ball.

Keep Up Your Pace

Make sure you are keeping up with the group of golfers ahead of you. If you are falling behind, consider limiting practice swings and shortening up the amount of time you search for lost balls, as discussed in the previous sections. If you have already hit a significant number of shots on a hole and you are holding up play, strongly consider picking up your ball instead of finishing the hole you are on. Be aware of how you are affecting the pace of play for the groups behind you.

Sand Traps

If you hit your ball into a sand trap, try to walk the shortest distance possible from the edge of the trap to your ball. You want to do the least amount of walking in the sand. Not only does this keep the trap well groomed, but it is also less raking for you to do after you have hit.

Once you are done hitting out of the trap, find a rake and smooth over your footprints and ball mark. Leave the rake at the edge of the trap when you are finished.

Replace Divots

Just as you did on the tee box, if your fairway shot takes a chunk of grass out of the ground, retrieve it and place it back over the bare spot you created. If the divot is too broken up and you have sand on the golf cart, place some sand over the spot before moving on.

Take Your Wedges And Putter

When you are playing shots that are next to the green and leaving your cart or bag, take your putter along with your wedges. The idea is to speed up play by avoiding multiple trips back and forth from the fringe/green to your bag. If you have your putter along with you, you can chip onto the green and quickly be ready to putt. Just remember to grab all of your clubs before leaving the green to head to the next hole!

On The Green

Repair Ball Marks

When you hit a shot from distance and it hits the putting green, it will leave a small dent. This is called a "ball mark". Depending on how hard you hit the green or how much moisture is in the ground, these marks can range from barely visible to quite significant.

Use a ball mark repair tool or a tee to repair any marks you may have created with your shot. If you spot any other unrepaired ball marks, fix those too. A good rule of thumb to follow is to try to leave the putting green in better shape than you found it.

Respect The Putting Lines

Each ball on the putting green has an imaginary path to the hole. This path is called the "line". You should never step on another player's line while you are on the green. When you are reading the green and lining up your own putt, be aware of all of the other player's lines and take care to step over or walk around them.

Order Of Play

Much like in the fairway or rough, the player who is farthest from the hole is "out" and will putt first. If multiple balls appear to be about the same distance away, whoever is ready should putt first. Get confirmation from your playing partners before you go first. If you are left with a short putt, your partners may allow you to "putt out". That is, they will let you finish up the hole without worrying about the strict order of play so that your ball is out of the way of others.

Mark Your Ball

If your ball is on or near the putting path of another player, mark your ball and move it out of the way. You can use a ball marker that lays flush to the green (often found in the clubhouse with the scorecards and pencils). Or you can stick a tee in the ground, making sure to move it several putter head lengths out of the way. When you are done marking your ball, always confirm with the player waiting to putt whether your mark is acceptable.

Watch Your Shadow

Be mindful of where you are casting a shadow on the green. Try to keep your shadow from covering the cup or other player's putting lines.

Gimmes

In friendly matches, it's customary to concede very short putts rather than making your playing partners putt them into the hole. These are called gimmes. You'll have to decide what an appropriate distance for a gimme is, but typically it's nothing longer than the length of a putter grip.

Be careful if you are playing in a competitive event or a tournament. Most of these require players to "hole out", so no gimmes are allowed!

The Flag

With the latest rule changes in golf, you are now allowed to keep the flag in the cup while putting.

Some players still prefer the flag to get pulled out. In that case ask them if they can see the cup from where they are putting. If they can't, they may ask you to "tend the flag". This means they want the flag to remain in the cup until after they have putted and then pulled out as the ball nears the cup. If you are asked to tend the flag, stand off to the side and grab hold of the flag stick, making sure to avoid standing on any putting lines. As the ball approaches the cup, pull the stick straight up and out.

If you have the flag out and on the ground, make sure it is far enough out of the way such that no missed putts will hit it. When everyone is done putting, remember to put the flag back in the hole.

Leave The Green Promptly

When you are done putting, promptly put the flag back in if you pulled it out, gather any clubs you might have left on the side of the green, and move out of the way. Wait until you are back at your cart and away from the hole before writing down scores, retrieving items from your bag, cleaning your clubs, or anything else. There may be a group behind you that is waiting to hit onto the green, so you want to get out of the way quickly.

Keep The Green Clean

Please don't spit anything on the greens, whether its sunflower seeds, tobacco, or anything else. When you're putting the last thing you want to deal with are objects in your putting line. Be respectful and just don't do it!

Spectator's Guide

At some point you may find that you want to attend a golf event as a spectator, whether it's a high school or college match, a club championship, a professional event, or just observing someone at a local course. Many of the rules that apply to playing golf also apply to watching it. Ultimately, it comes down to being respectful of the players you have come to watch.

Remain Quiet And Still During Shots

While watching a golf match, try to only talk to other spectators in between shots. While a player is setting up and addressing the ball, remain quiet and do not move around.

Remaining quiet applies to your phone as well, so make sure it is silenced. Having your phone ring in the middle of a player's swing is a quick way to get escorted out of an event! If you need to take a phone call, please walk away from hole before doing so.

Dress Code

If you know the dress code rules for playing golf, then you already know the rules for watching golf! Golf is a unique sport in that the spectators are typically dressed the same as the players. Collared shirts are the norm, along with either dress shorts or pants.

Bring The Right Gear

Check the forecast and bring the appropriate gear. If you will be out in the sun all day long, you'll likely want to bring sunglasses, a hat, and sunscreen. If there is a chance of rain, you may want to have an umbrella or rain coat along with you.

No Coaching

If you are watching a competition in which you know one of the competitors, you may be tempted to give out tips or advice during the round. Please remember, in most scenarios coaching during a round is not allowed. Don't risk getting your player disqualified by coaching them from the crowd!

Watch Out For Flying Golf Balls

Try to pay attention when players are hitting into an area near where you are standing. If you see a ball heading your way or you hear someone yell "Fore!!", cover your head and duck down.

Conclusion

I hope you now have a better understanding of the rules of etiquette in the game of golf! Remembering them all can take a bit of practice. But before long these rules will become second nature to you!

I encourage you to play several rounds with more experienced golfers and practice these rules. If you are ever unsure about something, don't hesitate to ask those you are playing with. And as you become more experienced yourself, remember to pay it forward! If you find yourself playing with a new golfer who is struggling with any of the rules of etiquette, politely offer them the advice you've learned over time. Most new golfers only break these rules unintentionally and may appreciate you lending them a helping hand.

I hope you found this guide informative and I wish you the best of luck in your golf journey!

Golf Terminology

Here is a brief list of some of the terms you might hear on a golf course, along with their meanings.

Ace: A hole in one! If you hit an ace, congratulations!

At The Turn: This refers to finishing Hole #9 (the end of the front nine) and starting off on Hole #10 (the beginning of the back nine). It is the halfway point when playing 18 holes.

Away: The player who is farthest from the pin, whether in the fairway/rough or on the green.

Backspin: The backward rotation of the golf ball, which typically causes the ball to quickly stop after landing and possibly even roll backwards if enough spin has been applied.

Birdie: A score of one under par on a hole. Shooting a 2 on a par 3 is an example of birdying the hole.

Bladed: Making contact on the ball with the bottom edge of an iron. This usually results in the ball flying much lower and farther than desired.

Bogey: A score of one over par on a hole. If you shoot a 5 on a par 4 hole, you have bogeyed the hole.

Bunker/Trap: A hazard on a course that is filled with sand, making it more difficult to hit out of.

Chunked: A shot in which you hit much more ground than you intended. A chunked shot will usually create a large divot and take a considerable bit of distance off the flight of the ball.

Dog Leg: A hole on a course in which the fairway goes out straight for a distance before making a sharp angle to the left or right.

Draw: A ball with a flight pattern that moves slightly right to left (if you are right-handed).

Eagle: A score of two under par on a hole. If you score a 3 on a par 5 hole, you have eagled the hole.

Fade: A ball with a flight pattern that moves slightly left to right (if you are right-handed).

Fairway: The section of grass between the tee box and putting green. The fairway has the most desirable length of grass from which to hit shots.

Fore: A warning golfers shout to alert others that a ball is heading in their direction and they should protect themselves.

Fringe: The first several mower cuts surrounding the putting green. The grass here is typically shorter than the fairway, but longer than the putting green itself.

Gimme: A short putt conceded to a player without having to actually make the putt.

Green: The shortest cut section of grass in which the cup resides.

Green Fee: The price paid to play on a golf course.

Honors: This refers to the player who had the lowest score on the last hole played. This person is said to "have honors" and has the right to tee off first.

Hook: A ball with a flight pattern that moves sharply to the left (if you are right-handed).

Lag (Putting): Hitting a putt from a long distance with the goal of not necessarily making the putt, but leaving it close enough to the cup to make the next putt.

Lie: The condition of how the ball is laying on the course. If the ball is buried in tall grass, you have a bad lie. If the ball is sitting up nicely in the fairway, you have a good lie.

Line (Putting): The desired path to the cup that a player wants the ball to follow on the putting green.

Mulligan: A do-over. Hitting another shot and disregarding the original.

Out Of Bounds: An area of a hole that is considered out of the field of play and therefore incurs a penalty stroke. You are not allowed to play a ball from an area that is deemed out of bounds.

Par: Shooting a score that matches the expected number of strokes for a hole. If you shot a 4 on a par 4, you have parred the hole.

Pin: The flag that sticks out of the cup on the green, marking where the cup is located.

Rough: This is the grass surrounding the fairway. It is the longest grass on the course and typically much more difficult to hit shots from.

Scramble: A type of team game in which each player hits a shot and then only the best shot is kept. Each player then hits the next shot from that spot.

Shank: A swing that makes contact with the ball on the very inside of the clubface, hitting the hosel (where the shaft is attached), and causing the ball to shoot out at an extreme angle. This is a word that many golfers are superstitious about, lest it happen to them, so refrain from using it on the golf course! You may even hear players refer to it as the "S-word" to avoid actually saying it!

Slice: A ball with a flight pattern that moves sharply to the right (if you are right-handed).

Snowman: Shooting a score of 8 on a hole. The number looks like a snowman!

The Tips: The tee box that is farthest back. The tips are usually only used by experienced, low handicap golfers.

Topped: Making poor contact with the ball such that you hit the top of it. A topped ball will usually not get much air under it or fly very far.

Yardage Marker: A measured and posted distance from somewhere on the course to the center of the green. Yardage might be marked with a colored post in the rough, a concrete marker in the fairway, or a distance labeled on a nearby sprinkler head. If a yardage marker uses colors, you can usually refer to your scorecard to find the color to distance mapping.

Made in United States
Orlando, FL
20 April 2022

16996821R10026